Elizabeth M. Potter / Beatrix Potter

Beatrix Potter painting book part 3

AF176095

by
Elizabeth M. Potter

Content   Page

Colouring pictures
I.   The Tale of the Pie and the Patty-Pan   3
II.   The Tailor of Gloucester   11
III. The Sly Old Cat   19
IV.   The Tale of Ginger and Pickles   27
V.   Original book illustrations   35
VI.   Further books of Elizabeth M. Potter   40

Bibliografische Information der Deutschen Nationalbibliothek:
Die Deutsche Nationalbibliothek verzeichnet diese Publikation in der Deutschen Nationalbibliografie; detaillierte bibliografische
Daten sind im Internet über http://dnb.dnb.de abrufbar.

© 2018 Elizabeth M. Potter 1. Auflage
Covergrafik, Texte und Bilder: © 2018 Elizabeth M. Potter

Herstellung und Verlag: BoD – Books on Demand, Norderstedt

ISBN: 9783752866377